The Unique
ONE-RECIPE
THREE-MEAL
Family Cookbook

The Unique
ONE-RECIPE
THREE-MEAL
Family Cookbook

SARA LEWIS

SMITHMARK

This edition published in 1996 by SMITHMARK Publishers
a division of U.S. Media Holdings, Inc.
16 East 32nd Street
New York, NY 10016

SMITHMARK books are available for bulk purchase
for sales promotion and premium use. For details
write or call the manager of special sales,
SMITHMARK Publishers, 16 East 32nd Street,
New York, NY 10016; (212) 532–6600.

ISBN 0-8317-7290-5

Produced by Anness Publishing Limited
1 Boundary Row
London SE1 8HP

This book was previously published as part of a larger
compendium, *Cooking for Babies and Toddlers*

Typeset by MC Typeset Ltd
Printed in Singapore by Star Standard Industries Pte. Ltd.

Publisher: Joanna Lorenz
Project Editors: Judith Simons and Emma Wish
Designer: Sue Storey
Special Photography: John Freeman
Stylist: Judy Williams
Home Economist: Sara Lewis

CONTENTS

INTRODUCTION

Eating together as a family takes on a new dimension as your family grows and there's a baby, fussy toddler and Mom and Dad to feed together. Rather than attempting to cook three different meals or to cook one very simple meal you know the children will like, opt instead to cook three meals

from one basic set of ingredients: a simple baby dinner, eye-catching meal for even the fussiest of toddlers and a spicy dinner for the grown-ups.

The recipes are aimed at a baby aged nine months and over, a toddler or small child aged eighteen months to four years and two adults.

Family Meals

Family meal times should be a pleasure but they can all too often turn into a battleground. Whatever family rules you have about table manners it's important that all the family knows about them and that you are consistent. What matters to some families may not be important to you. If you want your children to stay at the table until everyone has finished, make sure all the family understands this. Some parents may feel it's more relaxing if the children leave the table once they have finished, leaving the adults to eat the rest of their meal in relative peace. Whatever you decide, stick to it; don't be brow beaten by well-meaning grandparents or friends.

Try to eat together as a family at

Left: *Part of the fun of eating together is sharing the preparation, too. Children love helping in the kitchen, and this involves them in the meal from the very start.*

Below: *A relaxed but polite atmosphere will enhance enjoyment and consequently encourage good eating habits.*

hot coffee pot or hot casserole dish. Similarly, beware of tiny hands reaching out from the highchair to grab a mug of hot coffee or snatch at a sharp knife.

Offer a variety of foods at each meal, some foods you know your toddler and baby will like and foods that you like too so that everyone is happy. Offer very tiny portions of foods that are new or ones that your child is not very fond of and encourage your child to have at least one mouthful.

Encourage baby to feed himself with easy-to-pick-up finger foods. This gives the adults a chance to eat their food too. Don't worry about the mess until you get to the end of the meal.

For added protection when your toddler is eating at the table, use a wipe-clean place mat and cover the seat of a dining chair with a towel or dish towel. Better still buy a thin padded seat cover that is removable and machine washable but will tie on to the seat securely.

Children cannot bear to eat foods that are too hot, not just because they may burn their mouths, but because of the frustration. Not being

least once a day, even if you don't all eat the same food, so that your toddler can learn how to behave by watching the rest of the family. Explain to other members of the family that you are all setting the baby an example – a great way to get everyone on their best behavior, whatever their age.

It is never too early to encourage children to help: setting the table can become quite a game, especially if dolly or teddy has a place set too. Passing plates, bread and salt and pepper can be perilous to begin with but with a little practice becomes second nature. Transform a dull wet Monday dinner into a special occasion with a few flowers or candles (well out of reach of very tiny children) and pretty table mats and paper napkins for added decoration.

Try to avoid using a tablecloth with very young children as they can pull the cloth and everything with it onto the floor and themselves, with appalling consequences if there's a

Above: Setting the table is another task that children delight in, and another way to make them feel part of the family meal time.

Below: Even if the child is too young to have exactly the same food, sharing the table is important.

able to eat when the food is there and they are hungry can lead to great outbursts of temper. Many children actually prefer their food to be just lukewarm. Cool broccoli quickly by rinsing with a little cold water. Spoon hot stews onto a large plate so they cool quickly and always test the temperature of foods before serving to a child.

TABLE MANNERS

Toddlers can be incredibly messy, but try not to be too fussy and just wipe sticky hands and faces at the end of the meal. Enjoyment is the key. If your child is eating her meal with enthusiasm rather than style, then that is the most important part at the beginning – table manners will come as your child becomes more adept with a knife and fork.

Be understanding and flexible, small children have a lot to learn when they begin to join in with family meals. An active toddler has to learn how to sit still – quite an art in itself – how to hold a knife and fork and how to drink from a cup

Below and below right: *Never forget that food and eating are meant to be fun – don't discipline the child just for the sake of it, and don't impose adult rules too quickly.*

and somehow watch what everyone else is doing and join in too.

The baby has to adapt to sitting up to the table in his highchair and waiting for an adult to offer him a spoonful of food. Not surprisingly there can be a few tantrums and accidents, not to mention mess. Try not to worry. Offer a few finger foods after a bowl of ground foods so that the baby can feed himself, giving you a chance to finish your own meal and tidy up.

Above: *Good manners and sharing provide the perfect atmosphere for good eating – and will aid digestion, too!*

Left: *Unusual and varied environments, and the different types of food that go with them, provide huge additional pleasure, and will also help to familiarize your child with situations they will encounter later.*

TIPS

● Offer cubes of cheese at the end of a meal to help counteract the potentially harmful effects of any sugary foods eaten.

● Try to encourage children to eat more fruit. Cutting it into small pieces and arranging it on a plate can prove very inviting.

● Encourage children of all ages to drink whole milk, either cold, warm or flavored, as it is a valuable source of the fat-soluble vitamins A and D and the important mineral calcium, vital for healthy bones and teeth.

● If you reheat baby food in the microwave, make sure you stir it thoroughly and leave it to stand for a couple of minutes so any hot spots can even out. Always check the temperature before serving.

● Always make sure a baby is well strapped into a highchair and never leave children unattended while eating in case of accidents.

● Children love the novelty of eating somewhere different. If it's a nice day, why not have a picnic in the local park. If eating outside, pack children's food separately.

● Snacks can play a vitally important part in a young child's diet as their growth rate is so high it can be difficult to provide sufficient calories and protein at meal times alone.

● Make sure you coordinate main meals and snacks so that you serve different foods and so that the snacks won't take the edge off the child's appetite for the main meal of the day.

● Try to avoid candies or cakes and fatty chips.

● Offer slices of fresh fruit, a few raisins or dried apricots, squares of cheese, a fruit yogurt or milky drink, cream cheese or smooth peanut butter on toast.

● Make food fun and allow your child to choose where they eat the snack, e.g. in the camp in the garden or at the swings.

Choosing a Balanced and Varied Diet

FOR A BABY, AGE 9–18 MONTHS

Once your baby progresses to more varied puréed meals, you are really beginning to lay down the foundations for a healthy eating pattern which will take your baby through childhood.

It is vitally important to include portions of food from each of the four main food groups shown here per day. But do make sure that the types of food you choose are suitable for the age of your baby.

FOR A TODDLER

Give your child a selection of foods in the four main food groups daily:

Breads, grains and cereals: include three to four helpings of the following food items per day – breakfast cereals, bread, pasta, potatoes, rice.

Fruit and vegetables: try to have three or four helpings per day. Choose from fresh, canned, frozen or dried.

Meat and/or alternatives: one to two portions per day – meal – all kinds, including hamburgers and sausages, poultry, fish (fresh, canned or frozen), eggs (well-cooked), lentils and legumes (for example baked beans, red kidney beans, chickpeas), finely chopped nuts, smooth peanut butter and tofu.

Dairy foods: include 1 pint of milk per day or a mix of milk, cheese and yogurt. For a child who starts refusing milk, try flavoring it or using it in custards, ice cream, rice pudding or cheese sauce. A carton of yogurt or 1½oz of cheese have the same amount of calcium as 5oz of whole milk.

Above: *Cereals and grains, like bread, potatoes, pasta and rice.*

Above: *Fruit and vegetables, including frozen, dried and canned goods for a child.*

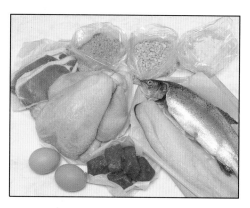

Above: *Meat and meat alternatives, like legumes and nuts (finely ground for a baby).*

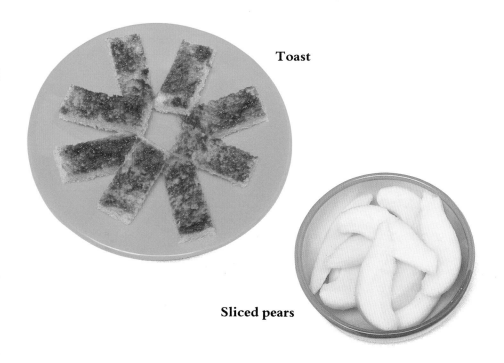

Above: *Dairy foods such as milk, cheese and yogurt (plain for a baby, at first).*

Toast

Sliced pears

FATS

As adults we are all aware of the need to cut down on our fat consumption, but when eating together as a family, bear in mind that fat is a useful source of energy in a child's diet. The energy from fat is in concentrated form, so that your child can take in the calories she needs for growth and development before her stomach becomes overfull. Fat in food is also a valuable source of the fat-soluble vitamins, A, D, E and K, as well as essential fatty acids that the body cannot make by itself.

In general, fat is best provided by foods which contain not just fat but other essential nutrients as well, such as dairy products, eggs, meat and fish. Whole milk and its products such as cheese and yogurt, and eggs contain the fat-soluble vitamins A and D, while sunflower oil, ground nuts and oily fish are a good source of various essential fatty acids.

Cut down on deep frying and broil or oven bake foods where possible. All children love chips and fries but do offer them as a treat rather than a daily snack.

FRUIT AND VEGETABLES
Fresh fruit and vegetables play an essential part in a balanced diet. Offer fresh fruit, such as slices of apple or banana, for breakfast and dinner, and perhaps thin sticks of carrot and celery for lunch. Instead of cookies and chips, offer your child raisins, ready-to-eat apricots, carrots and apple slices if she wants a mid-morning or afternoon snack. Keep the fruit bowl within easy reach so your child may be tempted to pick up a banana as she walks through the kitchen.

Above: *A good mixture of the four basic food types will provide maximum energy and vitality for growing children.*

SNACKS
Young children cannot eat enough food at meal times to meet their needs for energy and growth and snacks can play a vital part in meeting these needs. However offer chocolate cookies and chips only as a treat. They contain little goodness and are bad for the teeth. At meal times keep sweets out of sight until the main course has been eaten.

Above: *Offer sweets and chocolate only as treats – give fruit and vegetables as snacks.*

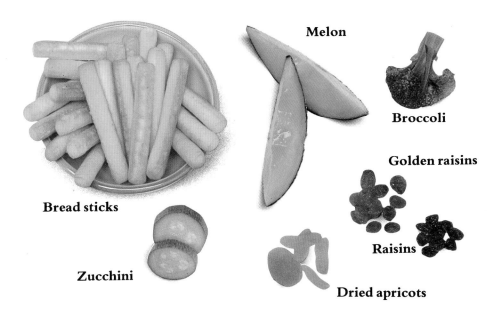

Bread sticks

Zucchini

Melon

Broccoli

Golden raisins

Raisins

Dried apricots

Coping With a Fussy Eater

We all have different sized appetites whatever our age, and young children are no exception. Children's appetites fluctuate greatly and often decrease just before a growth spurt. All children go through food fads; some just seem to last longer and be more difficult than others.

A toddler's appetite varies enormously and you may find that she will eat very well one day and eat hardly anything the next. Be guided by your toddler and try to think in terms of what the child has eaten over several days rather than just concentrating on one day.

At the time, it can be really frustrating and worrying. Try not to think of the food that you have just thrown away but try to think more of the long term. Jot down the foods that your child has actually eaten over three or four days or up to a week. You may actually be surprised, it's not just juice and chips after all!

Once you have a list you may find a link between the foods your child eats and the time of day. Perhaps your child eats better when eating with the family, or when the house is quiet. If you do find a link then build on it. You might find that your child is snacking on chocolate, doughnuts, soft drinks or fries when out with friends, and that fussiness at home is really a full tummy. Or it may be that by cutting out a milky drink and a cookie mid-morning and offering a sliced apple instead, your child may not be so full come lunch time. Perhaps you could hide the cookie box once visitors have had one, so that tiny hands can't keep reaching for more.

If your toddler seems hungrier at breakfast then you could offer eggy bread, a grilled sausage or a few banana slices with her cereal.

Above: *Don't panic about food rejection. Be patient and keep a journal listing what your child actually does eat.*

Right: *Fresh, healthful snacks will preserve the appetite for main meals.*

Although this all sounds obvious, when rushing about caring for a toddler and perhaps an older child or new baby, life becomes rather blurred and it can be difficult to stand back and look at things objectively.

REFUSING TO EAT

A child will always eat if she is hungry although it may not be when you want her to eat. A child can stay fit and healthy on surprisingly little. Providing your child is growing and gaining weight then don't worry, but if you are concerned, ask your doctor for advice. Take the lead from your child, never force feed a child and above all try not to let meal times become a battleground.

MAKING MEAL TIMES FUN

Coping with a fussy eater can be incredibly frustrating. The less she eats the angrier you get and so the spiral goes on as your toddler learns how to control meal times. To break this vicious circle, try defusing things by involving your child in the preparation of the meal. You could pack up a picnic with your child's help, choosing together what to take. Then go somewhere different to eat, it could be the back yard, the playground or even the car. Alternatively, have a dolls' or teddies' tea party or make a camp under the dining table.

Even very young children enjoy having friends for dinner. If your child is going through a fussy or non-eating stage, invite over a little friend with a good appetite. Try to take a back seat and don't make a fuss over how much the visiting child eats.

Above: *Changing the scene and breaking routine can help a lot.*

Below: *Making the meal a special event can distract the child from any eating worries.*

Above: *Getting your child to help you cook the food will encourage them to eat it, too.*

Above: *Children are more likely to eat with friends of their own age around them.*

10 TIPS TO COPE WITH A FUSSY EATER

1 Try to find meals that the rest of the family enjoys and where there are at least one or two things the fussy child will eat as well. It may seem easier to cook only foods that your child will eat but it means a very limited diet for everyone else and your child will never get the chance to have a change of mind and try something new.

2 Serve smaller portions of food to your child.

3 Invite her friend with a hearty appetite to dinner. A good example sometimes works but don't comment on how much the visiting child has eaten.

4 Invite an adult who the child likes for supper – a grandmother or friend. Sometimes a child will eat for someone else without any fuss at all.

5 Never force feed a child.

6 If your child is just playing with the food and won't eat, quietly remove the plate without fuss and don't offer dessert.

7 Try to make meal times enjoyable and talk about what the family has been doing.

8 Try limiting snacks and drinks between meals so your child feels hungrier when it comes to family meal times. Alternatively, offer more nutritious snacks and smaller main meals if your child eats better that way.

9 Offer drinks after a meal so that they don't spoil the appetite.

10 Offer new foods when you know your child is hungry and hopefully more receptive.

Above: *Remember to give drinks after the meal, not before.*

EATING TOGETHER

Eating together as a family should be a happy part of the day, but can turn into a nightmare if everyone is tired or you feel as though the only things your children will eat are fries.

There is nothing worse than preparing a lovely supper, setting the table and sitting down with everyone and then one child refuses to eat, shrieks her disapproval or just pushes the food around the plate. However hard you try to ignore this behavior, the meal is spoiled for everyone, especially if this is a regular occurrence. It's not fair on you or anyone else.

If you feel this is just a passing phase, then you could try just ignoring it and carry on regardless. Try to praise the good things, perhaps the way the child sits nicely at the table or the way she holds a knife and fork. Talk about the things that have been happening in the day, rather than concentrating on the meal itself. Try to avoid comparing your child's appetite with more hearty eaters. With luck, this particular fad will go away.

However, if it becomes a regular thing and meal times always seem more like a battleground than a happy family gathering, perhaps it's time for a sterner approach.

First steps
● Check to see if there is something physically wrong with your child. Has she been ill? If she has, she may not have recovered fully. If you're worried, then ask your doctor.
● Perhaps your child has enlarged adenoids or tonsils which could make swallowing difficult, or perhaps she has a food allergy, such as coeliacs disease – an intolerance to gluten – which may be undiagnosed but which would give the child tummy pains after eating. Again, check with your doctor.
● Is your child worried or stressed? If your family circumstances have changed – a new baby perhaps, or if you've moved recently – your child may be unhappy or confused.
● Is your child trying to get your attention?

Above: *Good seating of the right height will contribute to comfort and relaxation.*

Secondly

Look at the way in which you as a family eat. Do you eat at regular times? Do you sit down to eat or catch snacks on the run? Do you enjoy your food or do you always feel rushed and harassed? Children will pick up habits from their parents – bad as well as good. If you don't tend to sit down to a meal or you have the habit of getting up during meal times to do other jobs, then it's hard to expect the child to behave differently.

Finally

Talk things over with all the family. If you all feel enough is enough, then it's time to make a plan of action. Explain that from now on you are all going to eat together where possible, when and where you say so. You will choose the food, there will be three meals a day and no snacks. Since milk is filling and dulls the appetite, milky drinks will only be given after a meal; during the meal water or juice will be provided.

It is vitally important to involve all the family in this strategy so that there is no dipping into the cookie jar or raiding the pantry for chips after school. Make sure that the fussy eater is aware of what is going to happen and give a few days' notice so that the idea can sink in.

Once you have outlined your strategy, work out your menus and stick to them. Include foods your child definitely likes, chicken or carrots for instance, and obviously avoid foods your child hates although you could introduce some new foods for variety. Set yourself a time scale, perhaps one or two weeks, and review things after this period has elapsed.

PUTTING THE PLAN INTO ACTION

Begin your new plan of action when all the family is there to help, such as a weekend, and stick to it. Make a fuss of the plans so it seems more like a game than a prison sentence. Add a few flowers to the table or a pretty cloth to make it more special.

Begin the day with a normal breakfast but give the fussy eater the smallest possible portion. If the child eats it up then offer something you know your child likes, such as an apple, a few raisins or a fruit yogurt.

As the days progress, offer a cookie or chocolate milk as a treat.

Give plenty of encouragement and praise, but be firm if the child acts up. If she behaves badly, take her to a different room or to the bottom of the stairs and explain that the only food is that on the table. Sit down with the rest of the family, leaving the fussy eater's food on the table and try to ignore the child.

If the child changes her mind just as you're about to clear the table, then get the other members of the family to come back and wait until the fussy eater has finished.

Continue in this way with other meals. Don't be swayed if your child says she will eat her food watching TV or if she wants her dessert first. Explain that she must eat just like everyone else or go without.

If she begins to cry, sit her down in another room and return to the table. This is perhaps the hardest thing of all.

After a few days, there should be a glimmer of progress. Still offer tiny portions of food, followed by foods that you know your child will eat as a treat. Keeping to a plan like this is hard, but if all the family sticks together and thinks positively, then it is possible. Keep to the time span you decided, then suggest you all go to your local pizza or burger restaurant and let the fussy eater choose what she likes.

MEATY MAIN MEALS

TRYING TO PLEASE ALL THE FAMILY ALL OF THE TIME CAN BE A BIT OF A TALL ORDER, ESPECIALLY WHEN TRYING TO COOK TASTY MEALS ON A BUDGET. TRY THESE DELICIOUS NEW WAYS WITH QUICK-TO-COOK GROUND BEEF AND CHOPS, PLUS A SPEEDY STIR FRY, OR SLOW-COOK BEEF BOURGIGNON, BRAISED PORK OR LAMB CASSEROLE.

Mediterranean Lamb

3 rib lamb chops
12oz zucchini
½ yellow bell pepper
½ red bell pepper
3 tomatoes
1 garlic clove, crushed
1 tbsp clear honey
few sprigs of fresh rosemary, plus extra to garnish
1 tbsp olive oil
7oz can baked beans
salt and freshly ground black pepper
crusty bread, to serve

2 Season two of the chops for the adults with garlic, honey, rosemary and salt and pepper, and drizzle oil over the vegetables.

3 Cook under a hot broiler for 12–14 minutes, turning once, until the lamb is well browned and cooked through and the vegetables are browned.

5 Chop or process the remaining lamb with four slices of zucchini, two small pieces of pepper, two peeled tomato quarters and 1–2 tbsp of baked beans, adding a little boiled water if too dry. Spoon into a dish for the baby and test the temperature of the children's food before serving.

6 For the adult's portions, discard the cooked rosemary. Spoon the pan juices over the chops and garnish with fresh rosemary. Serve with crusty bread.

1 Rinse the chops under cold water, pat dry, trim off any fat and place in the base of a broiling pan. Trim and slice the zucchini, cut away the core and seeds from the peppers and then rinse and cut into chunks. Rinse and cut the tomatoes into quarters and arrange the vegetables around the lamb.

4 Warm the baked beans in a small saucepan. Drain and transfer the unseasoned chop to a chopping board and cut away the bone and fat. Thinly slice half the meat for the toddler and arrange on a plate with a few of the vegetables and 2–3 tbsp of the baked beans.

TIP
Lamb varies hugely in price throughout the year. Depending on the season and price you may prefer to use lamb cutlets or loin chops. Allow two chops per adult and reduce the cooking time slightly as these chops are smaller. Do not give honey to young children. Use red currant jelly in place of honey for children and adults if preferred.

Lamb Casserole

12oz boneless lamb

1 onion

1 carrot

6oz rutabaga

1 tbsp light vegetable oil

2 tbsp all-purpose flour

1⅞ cups beef broth

1 tbsp fresh sage or ¼ tsp
   dried sage

2oz chorizo (optional)

½ eating apple

10oz potatoes

1 tbsp butter

8oz Brussels sprouts

salt and freshly ground black pepper

1 Preheat the oven to 350°F. Rinse the lamb under cold water, pat dry, trim away any fat and then slice thinly. Peel and chop the onion, carrot and rutabaga.

2 Heat the oil in a large skillet and brown the lamb on both sides. Lift the lamb out of the pan, draining off any excess oil and transfer one-third to a small 2½ cup casserole dish for the children and the rest to a 5 cup casserole dish for the adults.

3 Add the vegetables to the pan and fry for 5 minutes, stirring until lightly browned.

4 Stir in the flour, then add the broth and sage. Bring to a boil, stirring, then divide between the two casserole dishes.

5 Peel and chop the chorizo if using, core, peel and chop the apple and add both to the larger casserole dish with a little seasoning.

6 Thinly slice the potatoes and arrange overlapping slices over both casserole dishes. Dot with butter and season the larger dish.

7 Cover and cook in the oven for 1¼ hours. For a brown topping, remove the lid and broil for a few minutes at the end of cooking until browned. Cook the Brussels sprouts in boiling water for 8–10 minutes until tender and drain.

8 Chop or process half the contents of the small casserole with a few sprouts for the baby, adding extra gravy if needed until the desired consistency is reached. Spoon into a baby dish.

9 Spoon the remaining child's portion onto a plate, add a few sprouts and cut up any large pieces. Test the temperature of the children's food before serving.

10 Spoon the adults' portions onto serving plates and serve with Brussels sprouts.

TIP
Traditionally, inexpensive stewing lamb would have been used for making a casserole. This cut does require very long slow cooking and can be fatty with lots of bones so not ideal for children. Boneless lamb is very lean, with very little waste and makes a tasty and healthier alternative.

Spicy Beef Sauté

12oz lean ground beef

1 onion, chopped

1 carrot, chopped

1 garlic clove, crushed

14oz can tomatoes

pinch of dried mixed herbs

1oz small pasta

2oz creamed coconut

2oz button mushrooms

2oz fresh spinach leaves

1 tbsp hot curry paste

salt and freshly ground black pepper

boiled rice, warm naan or other
    Indian bread and a little grated
    Cheddar cheese (optional), to serve

1 Brown the meat and onion in a
medium-sized dry saucepan,
stirring continuously.

2 Add the carrot, garlic, tomatoes
and herbs, bring to a boil,
stirring, and then cover and simmer
for about 30 minutes, stirring
occasionally.

3 Cook the pasta in a small
saucepan of boiling water for
10 minutes until tender. Drain.

4 Meanwhile place the coconut in
a small bowl, add ½ cup of
boiling water and stir until
dissolved. Wipe and slice the
mushrooms and wash and drain the
spinach, discarding any large stalks.

5 Transfer one-third of the meat
mixture to another saucepan.
Stir the coconut mixture, curry paste
and salt and pepper into the
remaining meat mixture and cook
for about 5 minutes, stirring.

6 Mash or process one-third of the
pasta and the reserved meat
mixture to the desired consistency
for baby and spoon into a small dish.

7 Spoon the remaining pasta and
reserved meat mixture into a
small bowl for the older child.

8 Stir the mushrooms and spinach
into the curried meat and cook
for 3–4 minutes until the spinach has
just wilted. Spoon onto warmed
serving plates for the adults and
serve with boiled rice and warmed
bread. Sprinkle the toddler's portion
with a little cheese, if desired. Test
the temperature of the children's
food before serving.

TIP
Weigh spinach after it has been
picked over and stalks removed or,
if you're short on time, buy ready
prepared spinach.
    If you can't get creamed coconut,
use ½ cup coconut milk instead.
Alternatively, soak 1 cup dried
coconut in ⅔ cup boiling water
for 30 minutes then strain and use
the liquid.

Ground Beef Curry

3 medium baking potatoes

1 onion, chopped

12oz lean ground beef

1 garlic clove, crushed

2 tsp mild curry paste

2 tsp wine vinegar

6 tbsp fresh breadcrumbs

1 tbsp tomato paste

1oz raisins

1 tbsp mango chutney

1 medium banana, sliced

2 eggs

4 tsp turmeric

½ cup skim milk

4 small bay leaves

8oz broccoli, cut into florets

2 tbsp fromage frais or plain yogurt

7oz can baked beans

salt and freshly ground black pepper

1 Preheat the oven to 350°F. Scrub the potatoes, insert a skewer into each and bake for 1½ hours until tender.

2 Place the chopped onion and 8oz of the beef in a saucepan and brown, stirring frequently.

3 Add the garlic and curry paste, stir well and cook for 1 minute, then remove from the heat and stir in the vinegar, 4 tbsp of the breadcrumbs, the tomato paste, raisins and a little salt and pepper.

TIP
Serve any leftover adult portions cold with salad.

4 Chop up any large pieces of mango chutney and stir into the meat mixture with the banana slices. Spoon into a 3¾ cup ovenproof dish and press into an even layer with the back of a spoon.

5 Place the dish on a baking sheet, cover loosely with foil and cook for 20 minutes.

6 Meanwhile mix the remaining beef with the remaining breadcrumbs, then beat the eggs together and stir 1 tbsp into the meat. Make eight small meatballs about the size of a grape for the baby. Form the remaining beef into a 3in patty using an upturned cookie cutter as a mold.

7 Blend the turmeric, milk and a little salt and pepper with the remaining eggs. Remove the foil from the ovenproof dish, and lay the bay leaves over the meat.

8 Pour the egg mixture over. Return to the oven for 30 minutes more until well risen and set.

9 When the adults' portion is ready, heat the broiler and cook the patty and meatballs until browned, turning once. The patty will take 8–10 minutes, while the meatballs will take about 5 minutes.

10 Cook the broccoli in boiling water until tender and drain.

11 Cut the adult portion into wedges and serve with baked potatoes topped with fromage frais or yogurt and broccoli.

12 Serve the toddler's patty with half a potato, warmed baked beans and a few broccoli florets. Serve the baby's meatballs with chunky pieces of peeled potato and broccoli. Spoon a few baked beans into a small dish for the baby. Test the temperature of the children's food before serving.

Moussaka

1 onion, chopped

12oz ground lamb

14oz can tomatoes

1 bay leaf

1 medium eggplant, sliced

2 medium potatoes

1 medium zucchini, sliced

2 tbsp olive oil

½ tsp grated nutmeg

½ tsp ground cinnamon

2 garlic cloves, crushed

salt and freshly ground black pepper

For the Sauce

2 tbsp margarine

2 tbsp all-purpose flour

1 cup milk

pinch of grated nutmeg

1 tbsp freshly grated Parmesan
cheese

4 tsp fresh breadcrumbs

1 Brown the onion and ground lamb in a dry saucepan, stirring occasionally. Add the tomatoes and bay leaf, bring to a boil, stirring, then cover and simmer for 30 minutes.

2 Place the eggplant slices in a single layer on a baking sheet, sprinkle with a little salt and set aside for 20 minutes. Preheat the oven to 400°F.

3 Slice the potatoes thinly and cook in boiling water for 3 minutes. Add the zucchini and cook for 2 minutes until tender.

4 Remove most of the slices with a slotted spoon and place in a colander, leaving just enough for the baby portion. Cook these for 2–3 minutes more until soft, then drain. Rinse the vegetables and drain well.

5 Rinse the salt off the eggplant and pat dry. Heat the oil in a skillet and brown the eggplant on both sides. Drain.

6 Spoon 3 tbsp of the meat mixture into a bowl with the baby vegetables and chop or purée to the desired consistency.

7 Spoon 4 tbsp of the meat mixture into an ovenproof dish for the older child with four slices of potato overlapping over the top, then add a slice of eggplant and three slices of zucchini.

8 Stir the nutmeg, cinnamon, garlic and seasoning into the remaining meat mixture, and cook for 1 minute and then spoon into a 5 cup shallow ovenproof dish discarding the bay leaf.

9 Arrange the remaining potatoes overlapping on top of the lamb, and then add the eggplant slices, tucking the zucchini slices in between the eggplant in a random pattern.

10 To make the sauce, melt the margarine in a small saucepan, stir in the flour then gradually add the milk and bring to a boil, stirring until thickened and smooth. Add a pinch of nutmeg and a little salt and pepper.

11 Pour a little of the sauce over the toddler's portion then pour the rest over the adults' portion. Sprinkle the larger dish with Parmesan cheese and 3 tsp breadcrumbs, sprinkling the remaining breadcrumbs over the toddler's portion.

12 Cook the moussakas in the oven. The larger dish will take 45 minutes while the toddler's portion will take about 25 minutes. Reheat the baby portion, and test the temperature of the children's food before serving.

Chili con Carne

3 medium baking potatoes

1 onion, chopped

1lb lean ground beef

1 carrot, chopped

½ red bell pepper, cored, seeded and diced

14oz can tomatoes

2 tsp tomato paste

⅔ cup beef broth

3 small bay leaves

2 tbsp olive oil

4oz button mushrooms, sliced

2 garlic cloves, crushed

2 tsp mild chili powder

½ tsp ground cumin

1 tsp ground coriander

7oz can red kidney beans, drained

1½oz frozen mixed vegetables

1 tbsp milk

pat of butter or margarine

4 tbsp fromage frais or plain yogurt

1 tbsp chopped fresh cilantro leaves

salt and freshly ground black pepper

green salad, to serve

1 Preheat the oven to 350°F. Scrub and prick the potatoes and cook in the oven for 1½ hours. Brown the onion and ground beef in a dry saucepan, stirring. Add the carrot and red pepper and cook for 2 minutes.

2 Add the tomatoes, tomato paste and broth and bring to a boil. Transfer one-quarter of the meat mixture to a 2½ cup casserole dish, add 1 of the bay leaves, cover with a lid and set aside.

3 Spoon the remaining meat mixture into a 5 cup casserole. Heat 1 tbsp of the oil in the same saucepan and sauté the mushrooms and garlic for 3 minutes.

4 Stir in the spices and seasoning, cook for 1 minute then add the drained red kidney beans and the remaining bay leaves and stir into the meat mixture. Cover and cook both dishes in the oven for 1 hour.

5 When the potatoes are cooked, cut into halves or quarters and scoop out the potato leaving a thin layer of potato on the skin.

6 Brush the potato skins with the remaining oil and broil for 10 minutes until browned.

7 Boil the frozen mixed vegetables for 5 minutes and mash the potato centers with milk and a pat of butter or margarine.

8 Spoon the meat mixture from the smaller casserole into an ovenproof ramekin for the toddler and the rest into a bowl for the baby. Top both with some of the mashed potato.

9 Drain the vegetables, arrange two pea eyes, carrot pieces for the mouth and mixed vegetables for hair on the toddler's dish.

10 Spoon the remaining vegetables into a baby bowl and chop or process to the desired consistency. Test the temperature of the children's food before serving.

11 Spoon the adults' chili onto serving plates, add the potato skins and top with fromage frais or yogurt and chopped cilantro. Serve with a green salad.

Beef Bourguignon with Creamed Potatoes

1lb stewing beef

1 tbsp light vegetable oil

1 onion, chopped

2 tbsp all-purpose flour

1¼ cups beef broth

1 tbsp tomato paste

small bunch of fresh herbs or ¼ tsp dried

2 garlic cloves, crushed

6 tbsp red wine

3oz shallots

3oz button mushrooms

2 tbsp butter

1lb potatoes

6oz green cabbage

2–4 tbsp milk

salt and freshly ground black pepper

a few fresh herbs, to garnish

1 Preheat the oven to 325°F. Trim away any fat from the stewing beef and cut into cubes.

2 Heat the oil in a skillet, add half of the beef and brown on all sides. Transfer to a plate and brown the remaining beef and the chopped onion.

3 Return the first batch of beef to the pan with any meat juices, stir in the flour and then add the broth and tomato paste. Bring to a boil, stirring, until thickened.

4 Spoon one-third of the beef mixture into a small 1¼ cup casserole dish for the children, making sure that the meat is well covered with broth. Add a few fresh herbs or half a dried bay leaf. Set the casserole aside.

5 Add the remaining herbs, garlic, wine and seasoning to the beef mixture in the skillet and bring to a boil. Transfer the beef to a 5 cup casserole dish. Cover both casserole dishes and cook in the oven for 2 hours or until the meat is very tender.

6 Meanwhile, cut the shallots in half if large, wipe clean and slice the mushrooms, then cover and set aside.

7 Half an hour before the end of cooking, sauté the shallots in a little butter until browned, then add the mushrooms and sauté for 2–3 minutes. Stir into the larger casserole and cook for the remaining time.

8 Cut the potatoes into chunks and cook in a saucepan of boiling, salted water for 20 minutes. Shred the cabbage, discarding the hard core, rinse and steam above the potatoes for the last 5 minutes.

9 Drain the potatoes and mash with 2 tbsp of the milk and the remaining butter.

10 Chop or process one-third of the child's portion with a spoonful of cabbage, adding extra milk if necessary. Spoon into a dish for the baby, with a little potato.

11 Spoon the remaining child's portion onto a plate for the toddler. Remove any bay leaf and cut up any large pieces of beef. Add potato and cabbage.

12 Garnish the adults' portion with fresh herbs and serve with potatoes and cabbage. Test the temperature of the children's food.

Braised Pork with Rice

3 pork spare rib chops, about
  1¼lb

1 tbsp olive oil

1 onion, chopped

1 large carrot, chopped

2 celery stalks, thinly sliced

2 garlic cloves, crushed

14oz can tomatoes

few sprigs fresh thyme or ¼ tsp
  dried thyme

grated zest and juice of ½ lemon

⅔ cup long grain rice

pinch of turmeric

4oz green beans

pat of butter

4 tbsp freshly grated Parmesan
  cheese

salt and freshly ground black pepper

1 or 2 sprigs parsley

1 Preheat the oven to 350°F. Rinse the chops under cold water and pat dry.

2 Heat the oil in a large skillet, add the pork, brown on both sides and transfer to a casserole dish.

3 Add the onion, carrot and celery to the skillet and sauté for 3 minutes until lightly browned.

4 Add half the garlic, the tomatoes, thyme and lemon juice and bring to a boil, stirring. Pour the mixture over the pork, cover and cook in the oven for 1½ hours or until tender.

5 Half fill two small saucepans with water and bring to a boil. Add ½ cup rice to one with a pinch of turmeric and salt, add the remaining rice to the second pan. Return to a boil, and simmer.

6 Trim the beans and steam above the larger pan of rice for 8 minutes or until the rice is tender.

7 Drain both pans of rice, and return the yellow rice to the pan and add the butter, Parmesan cheese and a little pepper. Mix together well and keep warm.

8 Dice one chop, discarding any bone if necessary. Spoon a little of the white rice onto a plate for the toddler and add half of the diced chop. Add a few vegetables and a spoonful of the sauce. Process the other half chop, some vegetables, rice and sauce to the desired consistency and spoon into a small bowl for the baby.

9 Spoon the yellow rice onto the adults' plates and add a pork chop to each. Season the sauce to taste and then spoon the sauce and vegetables over the meat, discarding the thyme sprigs if used. Finely chop the parsley and sprinkle over the pork with the lemon zest and the remaining crushed garlic.

10 Serve the adults' and toddler's portions with green beans. Test the temperature of the children's food before serving.

Pork Stir Fry

9oz pork fillet

1 zucchini

1 carrot

½ green bell pepper

½ red bell pepper

½ yellow bell pepper

7oz fresh bean sprouts

4 tsp light vegetable oil

1oz cashew nuts

⅔ cup chicken broth

2 tbsp ketchup

2 tsp cornstarch, blended with 1 tbsp
    cold water

1 garlic clove, crushed

2 tsp soy sauce

4 tsp yellow bean paste or
    hoisin sauce

1 Rinse the pork under cold water, cut away any fat and thinly slice. Halve the zucchini lengthwise and then slice thinly, thinly slice the carrot, and cut the peppers into thin strips, discarding the core and the seeds. Place the bean sprouts in a strainer and rinse well.

2 Heat 3 tsp of the oil in a wok or large skillet, add the cashews and sauté for 2 minutes until browned. Drain and reserve.

3 Add the sliced pork and stir fry for 5 minutes until browned all over and cooked through. Drain and keep warm.

4 Add the remaining oil and stir fry the zucchini and carrot for 2 minutes. Add the peppers and fry for 2 minutes more.

5 Stir in the bean sprouts, broth, ketchup and the cornstarch mixture, bring to a boil, stirring until the sauce has thickened.

6 Transfer 1 large spoonful of the vegetables to a bowl and 2–3 large spoonfuls to a plate for the children and set aside. Add the garlic and soy sauce to the pan and cook for 1 minute.

7 Chop or process four slices of pork with the baby's reserved vegetables to the desired consistency and spoon into a baby bowl. Arrange six slices of pork on the child's plate with the reserved vegetables. Spoon the vegetables in the wok onto two adult plates.

8 Return the remaining pork to the wok with the nuts and yellow bean paste or hoisin sauce and cook for 1 minute, spoon onto the adults' plates and serve immediately. Test the temperature of the children's food before serving.

Sausage Casserole

1lb large breakfast sausages
1 tbsp light vegetable oil
1 onion, chopped
8oz carrots, chopped
14oz can mixed navy and kidney beans in water, drained
1 tbsp all-purpose flour
1⅞ cup beef broth
1 tbsp Worcestershire sauce
3 tsp tomato paste
3 tsp brown sugar
2 tsp Dijon mustard
1 bay leaf
1 dried chili, chopped
3 medium baking potatoes
1 tbsp butter
salt and freshly ground black pepper
butter and sprigs of fresh parsley, to serve

1 Preheat the oven to 350°F. Prick and separate the sausages.

2 Heat the oil in a skillet, add the sausages and cook over high heat until evenly browned but not cooked through. Drain and transfer to a plate.

3 Add the chopped onion and carrots to the pan and sauté until lightly browned. Add the drained beans and flour, stir well and then spoon one-third of the bean mixture into a small casserole dish. Stir in ⅔ cup broth, 1 tsp tomato paste and 1 tsp sugar.

4 Add the Worcestershire sauce, remaining beef broth, tomato paste and sugar to the pan, together with the mustard, bay leaf and chopped chili. Season and bring to a boil, then pour the mixture into a large casserole dish.

5 Add two sausages to the small casserole dish and the rest to the larger dish. Cover both and cook in the oven for 1½ hours.

6 Scrub and prick the potatoes and bake on a rack above the casserole for 1½ hours until tender.

7 Spoon two-thirds of the child's casserole on to a plate for the toddler. Slice the sausages and give him or her two-thirds. Halve one of the baked potatoes, add a pat of butter and place on the toddler's plate.

8 Scoop the potato from the other half and mash or process with the remaining child's beans to the desired consistency for baby. Spoon into a dish and serve the remaining sausage slices as finger food.

9 Spoon the adults' casserole on to plates, halve the other potatoes, add butter and garnish with parsley. Test the temperature of the children's food before serving.

PERFECT POULTRY

WHATEVER THE AGE OF THE DINER, CHICKEN AND TURKEY ARE ALWAYS POPULAR. AVAILABLE IN A RANGE OF CUTS AND PRICES THERE'S SOMETHING TO SUIT ALL BUDGETS AND TASTES FROM A TASTY SALAD TO PAN-FRIED TURKEY, TANDOORI-STYLE MARINADE OR STUFFED CHICKEN BREASTS WITH PESTO, HAM AND CHEESE.

Chicken and Thyme Casserole

6 chicken thighs
1 tbsp olive oil
1 onion, chopped
2 tbsp all-purpose flour
1¼ cups chicken broth
few sprigs fresh thyme or ¼ tsp dried thyme
To Serve
12oz new potatoes
1 large carrot
¾ cup frozen peas
1 tsp Dijon mustard
grated zest and juice of ½ orange
4 tbsp fromage frais or plain yogurt
salt and freshly ground black pepper
few fresh thyme or parsley sprigs, to garnish

1 Preheat the oven to 350°F. Rinse the chicken thighs under cold water and pat dry.

2 Heat the oil in a large skillet, add the chicken and brown on both sides, then transfer to a casserole.

3 Add the onion and sauté, stirring until lightly browned. Stir in the flour, then add the broth and thyme and bring to a boil, stirring.

4 Pour over the chicken, cover and cook in the oven for 1 hour or until tender.

5 Meanwhile scrub the potatoes and cut any large ones in half. Cut the carrot into matchsticks.

6 Cook the potatoes in boiling water 15 minutes before the chicken is ready and cook the carrots and peas in a separate pan of boiling water for 5 minutes. Drain.

7 Take one chicken thigh out of the casserole, remove the skin and cut the meat away from the bone. Chop or process with some of the vegetables and gravy to the desired consistency. Spoon into a baby bowl.

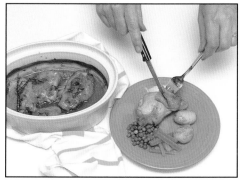

8 Take a second chicken thigh out of the casserole for the toddler, remove the skin and bone and slice if necessary. Arrange on a plate with some of the vegetables and gravy. Test the temperature of the children's food before serving.

9 Arrange the remaining chicken thighs onto warmed serving plates for the adults. Stir the mustard, orange zest and juice, fromage frais or yogurt and seasoning into the hot sauce and then spoon over the chicken. Serve at once, with the vegetables, garnished with a sprig of thyme or parsley.

Tandoori Chicken

6 chicken thighs

5oz plain yogurt

1¼ tsp paprika

1 tsp hot curry paste

1 tsp coriander seeds, roughly crushed

½ tsp cumin seeds, roughly crushed

½ tsp turmeric

pinch of dried mixed herbs

2 tsp light vegetable oil

To Serve

12oz new potatoes

3 celery stalks

4in piece cucumber

1 tbsp olive oil

1 tsp white wine vinegar

1 tsp mint jelly

salt and freshly ground black pepper

few sprigs of watercress, pat of butter and cherry tomatoes, to serve

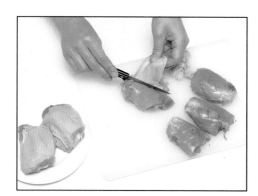

1 Cut away the skin from the chicken thighs and slash the meat two or three times with a small knife. Rinse under cold water and pat dry.

2 Place four thighs in a shallow dish, the other two on a plate. Place the yogurt, 1 tsp of the paprika, the curry paste, both seeds and almost all the turmeric into a small bowl and mix together. Spoon over the four chicken thighs.

3 Sprinkle the remaining paprika and the mixed herbs over the other chicken thighs and sprinkle the remaining pinch of turmeric over 1 thigh. Cover both dishes loosely with plastic wrap and chill in the refrigerator for 2–3 hours.

4 Preheat the oven to 400°F. Arrange the chicken thighs on a roasting rack set over a small roasting pan and drizzle oil over the herbed chicken. Pour a little boiling water into the base of the pan and cook for 45–50 minutes or until the juices run clear when the chicken is pierced with a skewer.

5 Meanwhile, scrub the potatoes and halve any large ones. Cook in a saucepan of boiling water for 15 minutes until tender.

6 Cut one celery stalk and a small piece of cucumber into matchsticks. Chop or shred the remaining celery and cucumber.

7 Blend together the oil, vinegar, mint jelly and seasoning in a bowl and add the chopped or shredded celery, cucumber and watercress, tossing well to coat.

8 Drain the potatoes and toss in a little butter. Divide the potatoes among the adults' plates, toddler's dish and the baby bowl. Cut the chicken off the bone for the toddler and arrange on a plate with half of the celery and cucumber sticks.

9 Cut the remaining chicken thigh into tiny pieces for the baby, discarding the bone. Add to the bowl with the cooled potatoes and vegetable sticks and allow baby to feed him- or herself. Add a few halved tomatoes to each portion. Test the temperature of the children's food before serving.

10 For the adults, arrange the chicken thighs on serving plates with the potatoes. Serve with the piquant salad.

Chicken Roll Ups

3 boneless, skinless chicken breasts

1 tsp pesto

1½oz thinly sliced ham

2oz Cheddar cheese

12oz new potatoes

6oz green beans

1 tbsp butter

2 tsp olive oil

1 tomato

6 pitted black olives

2 tsp all-purpose flour

⅔ cup chicken broth

1 tbsp crème fraîche or sour cream (optional)

few sprigs of fresh basil (optional)

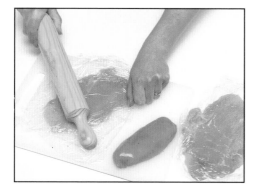

1 Rinse the chicken under cold water and pat dry. Put one chicken breast between two pieces of plastic wrap and pound with a rolling pin until half as big again. Repeat the process with the other two chicken breasts.

TIP
Depending on the age of your baby, you may prefer to omit the sauce and serve the meal as finger food, cutting it into more manageable pieces first.

2 Spread pesto over two of the chicken breasts and divide the ham among all three. Cut the cheese into three thick slices then add one to each piece of chicken. Roll up so that the cheese is completely enclosed, then secure with string.

3 Scrub the potatoes, halve any large ones and cook in a saucepan of boiling water for 15 minutes until tender. Trim the beans and cook in a separate pan of boiling water for 10 minutes.

4 Meanwhile, heat the butter and oil in a large skillet, add the chicken and sauté for about 10 minutes, turning several times, until well browned and cooked through.

5 Lift the chicken out of the pan, keeping those spread with pesto warm, and allowing the other one to cool slightly.

6 Cut the tomato into wedges and halve the olives. Stir in the flour and cook for 1 minute. Gradually stir in the broth and bring to a boil, stirring until thickened. Add the tomato and olives.

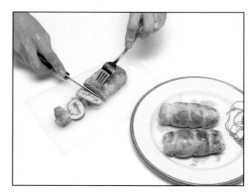

7 Snip the string off the chicken and slice the children's chicken breast thinly. Arrange four chicken slices on a child's plate with a couple of spoonfuls of sauce and a few potatoes and green beans. (Don't offer olives unless the child is a very adventurous eater.)

8 Chop or process the remaining cut chicken with 2 tbsp of the sauce, one or two potatoes and three green beans to the desired consistency. Test the temperature of the children's food before serving.

9 Arrange the remaining chicken on plates. Add the crème fraîche or sour cream to the pan, if using, and heat gently. Spoon over the chicken and serve with vegetables.

Pan-fried Turkey

3 large turkey cutlets

1 onion

1 red bell pepper, cored and seeded

1 tbsp light vegetable oil

1 tsp all-purpose flour

⅔ cup chicken broth

2 tbsp frozen corn

⅔ cup long grain white rice

1 garlic clove

1 dried chili

2oz creamed coconut

2 tbsp chopped fresh cilantro

fresh cilantro sprigs and lime
wedges, to serve

1 Rinse the turkey cutlets under cold water, and pat dry. Chop one of the cutlets, finely chop one-quarter of the onion and dice one-quarter of the red pepper. Heat 1 tsp of the oil in a small frying pan and sauté the diced turkey and chopped onion until browned.

2 Stir in the flour, add the broth, corn and chopped pepper, then bring to a boil, cover and simmer for 10 minutes.

3 Cook the long grain rice in boiling water for 8–10 minutes or until just tender. Drain.

4 Meanwhile process or finely chop the remaining pieces of onion and red pepper with the garlic and chili, including the seeds if you like hot food.

5 Put the creamed coconut into a bowl, pour on 1 cup boiling water and stir until the coconut is completely dissolved.

6 Heat the remaining oil in a large skillet. Brown the turkey cutlets on one side, turn over and add the pepper paste. Sauté for 5 minutes until the second side of the turkey is also browned.

7 Pour the coconut milk over the turkey and cook for 2–3 minutes, stirring until the sauce has thickened slightly. Sprinkle with the chopped fresh cilantro.

8 Chop or process one-third of the children's portion with 2 tbsp of the rice until the desired consistency is reached. Spoon into a baby bowl.

9 Spoon the child's portion onto a child's plate and serve with a little rice. Test the temperature of the children's food before serving.

10 Spoon the rest of the rice onto warmed serving plates for the adults, add the turkey and sauce and garnish with cilantro sprigs and lime wedges.

Chicken Salad

3 boneless, skinless chicken breasts

½ onion, chopped

1 carrot, chopped

⅔ cup chicken broth

few fresh herbs or a pinch of dried mixed herbs

2 tbsp butter or margarine

1 tbsp all-purpose flour

2 tbsp frozen corn, defrosted

3 slices bread

2 celery stalks

1 green eating apple

1 red eating apple

mixed salad greens and 1 small tomato, cut into wedges, to serve

For the Dressing

3 tbsp plain yogurt

3 tbsp mayonnaise

1 tsp ground coriander

salt and freshly ground black pepper

3 Strain the broth into a jug, finely chop the carrot and remove and discard the onion and herbs.

4 Preheat the oven to 375°F. Melt 1 tbsp of the butter or margarine in a small saucepan, stir in the flour and then gradually stir in the strained broth and bring to a boil, stirring until the sauce is thickened and smooth. Add the finely diced chicken, the chopped carrot and corn.

5 Cut the bread into three 3in squares, cutting the trimmings into tiny shapes using cutters. Spread both sides of the squares and one side of the tiny bread shapes with the remaining butter or margarine. Press the squares into sections of a muffin pan.

6 Bake the small shapes in the oven for 5 minutes and the squares for 10 minutes, until crisp and golden brown all over.

7 Rinse and thinly slice the celery, and quarter, core and chop half of each of the apples.

8 To make the salad dressing, blend the yogurt, mayonnaise, ground coriander and salt and pepper in a bowl. Add the thickly diced chicken and the celery, pepper and apples and mix together.

9 Tear the salad greens into pieces and arrange on the adults' serving plates. Spoon the chicken salad over the salad leaves.

10 Chop or process half of the child's chicken mixture to the desired consistency for the baby and spoon into a dish with the tiny bread shapes. Reheat the remaining mixture if necessary, spoon into the bread cases and arrange on a plate for the toddler. Slice the two apple halves, cutting the peel away from a few slices and add to the children's dishes. Check the temperature of hot food before serving to children.

1 Rinse the chicken breasts under cold water and place in a saucepan with the chopped onion and carrot, broth and herbs. Cover and cook for 15 minutes or until the chicken is cooked through.

2 Cut one chicken breast into small dice, cutting the other two into larger pieces.

FISH DINNERS

QUICK TO MAKE FOR EVERYDAY OR A SPECIAL OCCASION – HERE ARE SOME FISH RECIPES FOR ANY DAY OF THE WEEK. CHOOSE FROM FRESH, FROZEN OR CANNED FISH FOR ADDED CONVENIENCE. FORGET ABOUT PLAIN FISH FINGERS AND ENCOURAGE THE CHILDREN TO TRY HOMEMADE FISH CAKES WITH A TASTY SAUCE FOR THE ADULTS, PAELLA, EYE-CATCHING FISH PATTY SHELLS OR COLORFUL SALMON AND COD KABOBS.

Paella

14oz cod fillet

4oz shrimp or a mixture of cooked shrimp, mussels and squid

1 tbsp olive oil

1 onion, chopped

1 garlic clove, crushed

⅔ cup long grain white rice

pinch of saffron or turmeric

few sprigs of fresh thyme or pinch dried

8oz can tomatoes

½ red bell pepper, cored, seeded and chopped

½ green bell pepper, cored, seeded and chopped

2oz frozen peas

2 tbsp fresh chopped parsley

salt and freshly ground black pepper

1 Remove any skin from the cod and place the seafood in a strainer and rinse well with cold water.

2 Heat the oil in a skillet, add the onion and sauté until lightly browned, stirring occasionally. Add the garlic and ½ cup of the rice and cook for 1 minute.

3 Add the saffron or turmeric, thyme, two of the canned tomatoes, 1½ cups water and salt and pepper. Bring to a boil and cook for 5 minutes.

4 Put the remaining rice and canned tomatoes in a small saucepan with ⅓ cup water. Cover the pan and cook gently for about 5 minutes.

5 Add 1 tbsp of the mixed peppers and 1 tbsp of the frozen peas to the small pan, adding all the remaining vegetables to the large pan. Place 4oz of the fish in a metal strainer or steamer, cutting in half if necessary. Place above a small pan of boiling water, cover and steam for 5 minutes. Add the remaining fish to the paella in the large pan, cover the pan and cook for 5 minutes.

6 Add the seafood to the paella, cover the pan and cook for a further 3 minutes.

7 Stir the chopped parsley into the paella and spoon onto two warmed serving plates for the adults. Spoon half of the tomato rice mixture and half the fish onto a plate for the child and process the remaining fish and rice to the desired consistency for the baby. Spoon into a dish and check both children's meals for bones. Test the temperature of the children's food before serving.

Fish Cakes

1lb potatoes, cut into pieces

1lb cod fillet

3oz spinach leaves, cleaned and stemmed

5 tbsp whole milk

2 tbsp butter

1 egg

1 cup fresh breadcrumbs

1oz drained sun-dried tomatoes

1oz drained stuffed olives

4oz plain yogurt

3 tomatoes, cut into wedges

½ small onion, thinly sliced

1 tbsp frozen peas, cooked

light vegetable oil, for frying

salt and pepper

lemon wedges and green salad, to serve

1 Half fill a large saucepan or steamer base with water, add the potatoes and bring to a boil. Place the cod in a steamer top or in a colander above the saucepan. Cover and cook for 8–10 minutes or until the fish flakes easily when pressed.

2 Take the fish out of the steamer and place on a plate. Add the spinach to the steamer, cook for 3 minutes until just wilted and transfer to a dish. Test the potatoes, cook for 1–2 minutes more if necessary, then drain and mash with 2 tbsp of the milk and the butter.

3 Peel away the skin from the fish, and break into small flakes, carefully removing any bones. Chop the spinach and add to the potato with the fish.

4 For baby, spoon 3 tbsp of the mixture into a bowl and mash with another 2 tbsp milk. Add a little salt and pepper, if desired, to the remaining fish mixture.

5 For the older child, shape three tablespoons of mixture into three small rounds with floured hands. For adults, shape the remaining mixture into four cakes.

TIP
Make sure you remove all bones from the fish.

6 Beat the egg and the remaining milk on a plate. Place the breadcrumbs on a second plate and dip both the toddler and the adult fish cakes first into the egg and then into the crumb mixture.

7 Chop the sun-dried tomatoes and stuffed olives and stir into the yogurt with a little salt and pepper. Spoon into a small dish.

8 Heat some oil in a skillet and fry the small cakes for 2–3 minutes each side until browned. Drain well and arrange on a child's plate. Add tomato wedges for tails and peas for eyes.

9 Brown the adult fish cakes in more oil if necessary for 3–4 minutes each side until heated through. Drain and serve with the dip, lemon and tomato wedges, thinly sliced onion and a green salad. Reheat the baby portion if necessary but test the temperature of the children's food before serving.

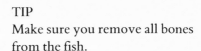

Fish Patty Shells

9oz puff pastry, thawed if
frozen

a little flour

beaten egg, to glaze

12oz cod fillet

⅓ cup milk

½ leek

2 tbsp margarine

2 tbsp all-purpose flour

2oz fresh shrimp

salt and pepper

broccoli, young carrots and snow
peas, to serve

1 Preheat the oven to 425°F. Roll out the pastry on a lightly floured work surface to make a 9 × 6in rectangle. Cut the pastry into three 3in wide strips.

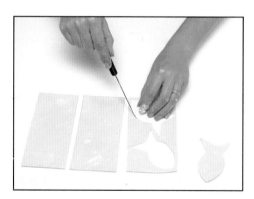

2 Cut two fish shapes from one strip. Neaten the edges with a knife and cut an oval shape in each "fish" just in from the edge and almost through to the bottom of the pastry. Place the fish shapes on a moistened baking tray.

TIP
You may find it easier to cut a fish shape out of paper and then use this as a template on the pastry.

3 Neaten the edges of one of the remaining pastry strips then cut a smaller rectangle ½in in from the edge and remove.

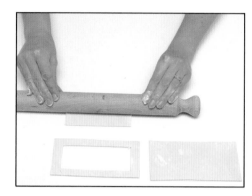

4 Roll out the smaller rectangle to the same size as the pastry frame. Brush the edges with a little egg and place the frame on top.

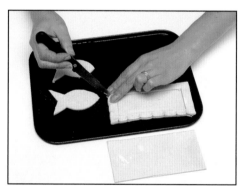

5 Transfer to the baking sheet. Neaten the edges of the rectangle with a small knife and flute between two fingers. Repeat the whole process with the third strip of pastry.

6 Stamp out tiny fish shapes from the pastry trimmings, rerolling if necessary, and place on the baking sheet. Brush the top of the patty shells with beaten egg and cook for 10 minutes, remove the small fish and cook the larger patty shells for 5 minutes more until they are well risen and golden brown.

7 Meanwhile make the filling. Cut the fish in half and put in a saucepan with the milk. Halve the leek lengthwise, wash thoroughly then slice and add to the pan.

8 Cover and simmer for 6–8 minutes or until the fish flakes easily when pressed with a knife. Lift out of the pan, peel away the skin and then break into pieces, removing and discarding any bones.

9 Strain the milk, reserving the leeks. Melt the margarine, stir in the flour and then gradually add in the milk and bring to a boil, stirring until thick and smooth.

10 Stir the fish into the sauce. Scoop out the centers of the fish-shaped patty shells and fill with a little mixture. Spoon 2 tbsp of fish mixture into a baby bowl.

11 Add a shrimp to each fish-shaped patty shell and stir the rest into the saucepan with the leeks and a little seasoning. Heat gently and spoon into the two large pastry cases. Transfer to plates and serve with steamed vegetables.

12 Chop the baby portion with some vegetables and serve this with some tiny pastry fish, if wished, in a small bowl. Check the temperature of the children's food before serving.

Salmon and Cod Kabobs

7oz salmon steak

10oz cod fillet

3 tsp lemon juice

2 tsp olive oil

½ tsp Dijon mustard

salt and freshly ground black pepper

12oz new potatoes

7oz frozen peas

4 tbsp butter

1–2 tbsp milk

3 tomatoes, chopped and seeded

¼ head iceberg lettuce, finely shredded

For the Mustard Sauce

1 sprig fresh dill

4 tsp mayonnaise

1 tsp Dijon mustard

1 tsp lemon juice

½ tsp dark brown sugar

1 Rinse the fish under cold water and pat dry. Cut the salmon steak in half, cutting around the central bone. Cut away the skin and then cut into chunks making sure you remove any bones. Remove the skin from the cod and cut into similar sized pieces.

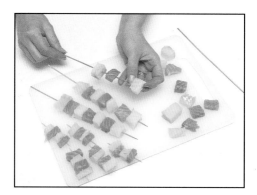

2 Cut a few pieces of fish into smaller pieces and thread onto five toothpicks. Thread the remaining fish pieces onto long wooden skewers.

3 Mix together the lemon juice, oil, Dijon mustard and a little salt and pepper to taste in a small bowl and set aside.

4 Finely chop the dill and place in a bowl with the other sauce ingredients and mix. Set aside.

5 Scrub the potatoes, halve any large ones and then cook in lightly salted water for 15 minutes or until tender. Place the peas and half of the butter in a skillet, cover and cook very gently for 5 minutes.

6 Preheat the broiler, place the kabobs on a baking sheet and brush the larger kabobs with the lemon, oil and mustard mixture. Broil for 5 minutes, until the fish is cooked, turning once.

7 Remove the fish from two toothpicks and mix in a small bowl with a few new potatoes and 1 tbsp of the peas. Chop or process with a little milk until the desired consistency is reached, then transfer to a baby bowl.

8 Arrange the toddler's kabobs on a small serving plate with a few potatoes, 2 tbsp peas and a small amount of chopped tomato. Test the temperature of the children's food before serving.

9 Add the tomatoes to the remaining peas and cook for 2 minutes, stir in the shredded lettuce and cook for 1 minute. Spoon onto serving plates for the adults, add the kabobs and potatoes and serve.

TIP
Depending on the age of the toddler, you may prefer to remove the toothpicks before serving.

Tuna and Spinach

2oz small pasta

6oz fresh spinach leaves

2oz frozen mixed vegetables

7oz can tuna in water

2 eggs

buttered toast and grilled tomatoes, to serve

For the Sauce

2 tbsp margarine

3 tbsp all-purpose flour

1¼ cups milk

½ cup grated Cheddar cheese

1 Cook the pasta in a pan of boiling water for 10 minutes. Meanwhile remove any spinach stalks, wash the leaves in plenty of cold water and place in a steamer or metal colander.

2 Stir the frozen vegetables into the pasta as it is cooking, and then place the spinach in the steamer over the top. Cover and cook for the last 3 minutes or until the spinach has just wilted.

TIP
Frozen vegetables are usually as nutritious as fresh vegetables since they are frozen at their peak of perfection – they're a great time saver too.

3 Drain the pasta and vegetables through a strainer. Chop one-quarter of the spinach and add to the pasta and vegetables, dividing the remaining spinach between two shallow 1¼ cup ovenproof dishes for the adults.

4 Drain the tuna and divide among the dishes and sieve.

5 Refill the pasta pan with water, bring to a boil then break the eggs into the water and gently simmer until the egg whites are set. Remove the eggs with a slotted spoon, trim the whites and shake off all the water. Arrange the eggs on top of the tuna for the adults.

6 To make the sauce, melt the margarine in a small saucepan, stir in the flour, then gradually add the milk and bring to a boil, stirring until thickened and smooth.

7 Stir the cheese into the sauce, reserving a little for the topping. Spoon the sauce over the adults' portions until the eggs are covered. Stir the children's pasta, vegetables and tuna into the remaining sauce and mix together.

8 Spoon the pasta onto a plate for the toddler and chop or process the remainder for baby, adding a little extra milk if necessary to make the desired consistency. Spoon into a dish. Test the temperature of the children's food before serving.

9 Preheat the broiler, sprinkle the adults' portions with the reserved cheese and grill for 4–5 minutes until browned. Serve with buttered toast and broiled tomatoes.

VEGETABLE FEASTS

MORE AND MORE OF US ARE OPTING TO EAT LESS MEAT FOR EITHER HEALTH OR BUDGET REASONS. EATING LESS MEAT DOESN'T MEAN LOSING OUT ON FLAVOR: FAR FROM IT! CHOOSE FROM MEALS SUCH AS TOASTED CHEESE SANDWICHES, CHEESE AND VEGETABLE CRISP OR SLOW-COOKED SPICED MOROCCAN VEGETABLE STEW.

Toasted Cheese Sandwiches

2 slices thick bread
2 slices thin bread
butter or margarine, for spreading
1 tsp Marmite or mild mustard
2 slices thinly sliced ham
1 garlic clove, halved
1 tbsp olive oil
7oz Cheddar cheese
1 tomato
6 pitted black olives
1 tbsp chopped fresh basil
a few red onion slices
cucumber sticks and green salad, to serve (optional)

2 Drizzle the oil over the thick slices of toast then rub with the cut surface of the garlic.

4 Slice the tomato and halve the olives. Arrange on the thick toast for the adults, season with pepper and add basil and onion.

3 Thinly slice the cheese and place over all of the pieces of toast.

5 Broil until the cheese is bubbly. Cut the plain toasted cheese into tiny squares, discarding crusts. Arrange on a small plate for baby and allow to cool. Cut the ham and cheese toast into triangles and arrange on a plate. Add cucumber sticks to the toddler's portion and test the temperature before serving.

1 Toast all the bread and spread the thin slices with butter or margarine. Spread one slice with Marmite or mild mustard and top this with ham.

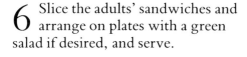

6 Slice the adults' sandwiches and arrange on plates with a green salad if desired, and serve.

Noodles with Tomato Sauce

5oz penne

1 onion

2 celery stalks

1 red bell pepper

1 tbsp olive oil

1 garlic clove, crushed

14oz can tomatoes

½ tsp superfine sugar

8 pitted black olives

2 tsp pesto

¼ tsp dried chili seeds
(optional)

½ cup grated Cheddar cheese

salt and freshly ground black pepper

2 tsp freshly grated Parmesan cheese,
to serve

green salad, to serve (optional)

2 Meanwhile chop the onion and the celery. Cut the pepper in half, then scoop out the core and seeds and dice the pepper finely.

3 Heat the oil in a large skillet, add the vegetables and garlic and sauté for 5 minutes, stirring until lightly browned.

6 Spoon 3–4 tbsp of the pasta mixture into a bowl or food processor and chop or process to the desired consistency for the baby. Spoon 5–6 tbsp of the pasta mixture into a bowl for the toddler.

1 Cook the pasta in salted boiling water for about 10–12 minutes until just tender.

4 Add the tomatoes and sugar and cook for 5 minutes, stirring occasionally until the tomatoes are broken up and pulpy.

5 Drain the pasta, return to the pan and stir in the tomato sauce.

7 Quarter the olives and stir into the remaining pasta with the pesto, chili seeds if using, and a little salt and pepper. Spoon into dishes.

8 Sprinkle the grated Cheddar cheese over all the dishes, and serve the adults' portions with the Parmesan cheese and a green salad, if wished. Test the temperature of the children's food before serving.

Zucchini Puff

4 tbsp butter

¼ cup all-purpose flour

2 eggs

½ tsp Dijon mustard

4oz Cheddar cheese

salt and pepper

For the Filling

1 tbsp olive oil

12oz zucchini, sliced

1 small onion, chopped

4oz button mushrooms, sliced

8oz tomatoes, skinned and chopped

1 garlic clove, crushed

4 tsp chopped fresh basil

1 Preheat the oven to 425°F and grease a large baking sheet. Place the butter in a medium-sized saucepan with ⅔ cup water. Heat gently until the butter has melted then bring to a boil.

2 Remove the pan from the heat and quickly add the flour, stir well then return to the heat and cook for 1–2 minutes, stirring constantly until the mixture forms a smooth ball. Let cool for 10 minutes.

3 Beat the eggs, mustard and a little salt and pepper together. Cut 1oz of the cheese into small cubes and grate the rest.

4 Add 2oz of the grated cheese to the dough and then gradually beat in the eggs to make a smooth, glossy paste.

5 Spoon the mixture into a large pastry bag fitted with a medium plain tube. Pipe whirls close together on the baking sheet to make a 7in circular shape.

6 Pipe the remaining mixture into small balls for the baby and into the older child's initials.

7 Sprinkle the dough shapes with the remaining grated cheese.

8 Bake for 15–18 minutes for the small shapes and 25 for the ring, until well risen and browned.

9 Heat the oil in a frying pan, add the zucchini and onion and sauté until lightly browned. Add the mushrooms, fry for a further 2 minutes and then add the tomatoes. Cover and simmer for 5 minutes until the vegetables are cooked.

10 Spoon a little mixture into the baby's bowl or into a food processor and chop or process to the desired consistency. Serve with a few cheese balls and a little diced cheese.

11 Spoon a little onto a plate for the toddler, add a cheese initial and the remaining diced cheese. Test the temperature of the children's food before serving.

12 Transfer the cheese ring to a serving plate and split in half horizontally. Stir the garlic, basil and a little extra seasoning into the courgette mixture and heat through. Spoon over the bottom half of the cheese ring and add top half. Serve the puff immediately.

TIP
Beat the flour and butter mixture, cheese and eggs in a food processor if preferred.

Cheese and Vegetable Crisp

1 onion

8oz carrot

6oz rutabaga

6oz parsnip

1 tbsp olive oil

7½oz can red kidney beans

2 tsp paprika

1 tsp ground cumin

1 tbsp all-purpose flour

1¼ cups vegetable broth

8oz broccoli, to serve

For the Topping

4oz Cheddar cheese

2oz whole wheat flour

2oz all-purpose flour

2oz margarine

2 tbsp sesame seeds

1oz blanched almonds

salt and freshly ground black pepper

1 Preheat the oven to 375°F. Peel and coarsely chop the onion and peel and cut the carrot, rutabaga and parsnip into small cubes. Heat the oil in a large pan and sauté the vegetables for 5 minutes, stirring until lightly browned.

2 Drain the kidney beans and add to the pan with the spices and flour. Stir well, add the broth, then cover and simmer for 10 minutes.

3 Meanwhile make the topping. Cut a few squares of cheese for the baby and grate the rest. Put the two flours in a bowl, add the margarine and rub in with your fingertips until the mixture resembles fine breadcrumbs. Stir in the grated cheese and sesame seeds.

4 Spoon a little of the vegetable mixture into a 1¼ cup ovenproof dish for the toddler. Spoon the remaining mixture into a 3¾ cup ovenproof pie plate for the adults, leaving a little vegetable mixture in the pan for the baby. Season the adults' portion with a little salt and pepper.

VARIATION
Lentil and Herb Crumble
Substitute canned lentils for the red kidney beans. Instead of the paprika and cumin, use 2 tbsp chopped, fresh mixed herbs. Add more fiber and texture by replacing the all-purpose flour with rolled oats.

5 Spoon 3 tbsp of the topping over the older child's portion. Coarsely chop the almonds, add to the remaining topping with a little salt and pepper and spoon over the large plate. Bake in the oven for 20 minutes for the small dish, 30 minutes for the large plate, until golden brown on top.

6 Add ⅓ cup water to the baby's portion, cover and cook for 10 minutes, stirring occasionally, until the vegetables are very tender. Mash or process to the desired consistency and spoon into a bowl.

7 Cut the broccoli into florets and cook for 5 minutes or until tender; drain. Spoon the toddler's portion out of the dish and onto a small plate. Serve the broccoli to all members of the family, allowing baby to pick up and eat the broccoli and cubed cheese as finger food. Check the temperature of the children's food before serving.

Note: Never give whole nuts to children under 5 as they may choke.

Moroccan Vegetable Stew

1 onion

8oz carrots

8oz rutabaga

3oz prunes

4 tsp olive oil

15oz can chickpeas

½ tsp turmeric

2 tsp all-purpose flour, plus extra for dusting

2 garlic cloves, finely chopped

1⅞ cups chicken broth

1 tbsp tomato paste

¾in piece fresh gingerroot

½ tsp ground cinnamon

3 cloves

4oz couscous

8 green beans

2 frozen peas

piece of tomato

pat of butter or margarine

salt and freshly ground black pepper

sprig fresh cilantro, to garnish

1 Peel and chop the onion and peel and dice the carrots and rutabaga. Cut the prunes into chunks, discarding the pits.

2 Heat 3 tsp of the olive oil in a large saucepan, add the onion and sauté until lightly browned. Stir in the carrots and rutabaga and sauté for 3 minutes, stirring.

3 Drain the chickpeas and stir into the pan with the turmeric, flour and garlic. Add 1¼ cup of the broth, the tomato paste, and the chopped prunes. Bring to a boil, cover and simmer for 20 minutes, stirring occasionally.

4 Place three heaping spoonfuls of mixture in a bowl or food processor, draining off most of the liquid. Mash or process and then form the mixture into a patty with floured hands.

5 Chop or process two heaping spoonfuls of mixture and sauce to the desired consistency for the baby and spoon into a bowl.

6 Finely chop the gingerroot and stir into the remaining vegetable mixture with the cinnamon, cloves, remaining broth and seasoning.

7 Place the couscous in a strainer, rinse with boiling water and fluff up the grains with a fork. Place the strainer above the vegetables, cover and steam for 5 minutes.

8 Brown the patty in the remaining oil on both sides. Trim and cook the beans and peas for 5 minutes. Drain and arrange on a plate like an octopus with a piece of tomato for a mouth and peas for eyes.

9 Stir the butter or margarine into the couscous and fluff up the grains with a fork. Spoon onto warmed serving plates for adults, add the vegetable mixture and garnish with a sprig of cilantro. Check the temperature of the children's food before serving.

Cheese and Leek Quiche

1½ cups all-purpose flour
6 tbsp butter
1 carrot
2 slices ham
4in piece of cucumber
mixed salad greens, to serve
For the Filling
2 tbsp butter
4oz trimmed leek, thinly sliced
3oz Stilton cheese, diced
1½oz Cheddar cheese, grated
3 eggs
¾ cup milk
pinch of paprika
salt and pepper

1 Put the flour in a bowl with a pinch of salt. Cut the butter into pieces and rub into the flour with your fingertips until the mixture resembles fine breadcrumbs.

2 Mix to a smooth dough with 6–7 tsp water, knead lightly and roll out thinly on a floured surface. Use to line a 7in pie pan, trimming around the edge and reserving the trimmings.

3 Reroll the trimmings and then cut out six 3in circles using a fluted cookie cutter. Press the pastry circles into sections of a muffin pan and chill all of the quiches.

4 Preheat the oven to 375°F. For the filling melt the butter in a small skillet and sauté the leek for 4–5 minutes, until soft but not brown, stirring frequently. Spoon into a bowl, stir in the diced Stilton, and then spread over the base of the large quiche.

5 Beat the eggs and milk together in a small bowl and season with salt and pepper.

6 Divide the grated Cheddar among the small quiche shells and pour some of the egg mixture over. Pour the remaining egg mixture over the leek and cheese quiche and sprinkle with paprika.

7 Cook the small quiches for 15 minutes and the large quiche for 30–35 minutes until well risen and browned. Leave to cool.

8 Peel and coarsely grate the carrot. Cut the ham into triangles for "sails". Cut the ham trimmings into small strips for the baby. Cut the cucumber into batons.

9 Place a spoonful of carrot, some cucumber, a small quiche and some ham trimmings in the baby dish. Spread the remaining carrot onto a plate for the older child, place the quiches on top and secure the ham "sails" with toothpicks. Serve any remaining quiches next day. Cut the large quiche into wedges and serve with the salad.

JUST DESSERTS

No one can resist a dessert, although looking after a young family may mean it's more of a weekend treat than an everyday occurrence. Spoil the family with a selection of these tasty hot and cold treats from fruity Berry Pudding and Plum Crumble to Chocolate and Tangerine Trifle or Orange and Strawberry Shortcakes – all guaranteed to get them clamoring for seconds.

Bread and Butter Pudding

3 dried apricots
3 tbsp golden raisins
2 tbsp sherry
7 slices white bread, crusts removed
½ tbsp butter, softened
2 tbsp superfine sugar
pinch of ground cinnamon
4 eggs
1¼ cups milk
few drops of vanilla extract
light cream, to serve

2 Preheat the oven to 375°F. Lightly spread the bread with butter and cut one slice into very small triangles. Layer the triangles of bread in a ⅔ cup pie plate with the plain apricots and raisins and 1 tsp of the sugar.

4 Beat the eggs, milk and vanilla together and pour into the ramekin and two pie plates.

1 Chop two dried apricots and place in a small bowl with 2 tbsp of the raisins and the sherry. Set aside for about 2 hours. Chop the remaining apricot and mix with the remaining raisins.

3 Cut the remaining bread into larger triangles and layer in a 3¾ cup pie plate with the remaining fruits and all but 1 tsp of the remaining sugar, sprinkling the top with cinnamon. Put the last 1 tsp sugar in a small ramekin.

5 Stand the ramekin in a large ovenproof dish and half fill with hot water. Cook the small pie plate and the ramekin for 25–30 minutes until the custard is just set, the larger pudding for 35 minutes until the bread is browned. Serve the adult portions with cream, if desired.

Berry Pudding

1¼lb cooking apples

¼ cup superfine sugar

2oz frozen or canned blackberries

For the Topping

4 tbsp butter or margarine

¼ cup superfine sugar

⅓ cup self-rising flour

1 egg

½ lemon, zest only

1 tbsp lemon juice

confectioner's sugar, for dusting

custard, to serve

1 Preheat the oven to 350°F. Peel and slice the cooking apples, discarding the core, and then place in a saucepan with the superfine sugar and 1 tbsp water. Cover and cook gently for 5 minutes until the apple slices are almost tender but still whole.

2 Half fill a ⅔ cup ovenproof ramekin with apple for the toddler and mash 2 tbsp apple for the baby in a small bowl.

3 Put the remaining apple slices into a 2½ cup ovenproof dish. Sprinkle the blackberries over the apple slices.

4 To make the topping, place the butter or margarine, sugar, flour and egg in a bowl and beat until smooth. Spoon a little of the pudding mixture over the toddler's ramekin so that the mixture is almost to the top of the dish.

5 Half fill three fluted paper baking cups with the pudding mixture.

6 Grate the lemon zest and stir with the juice into the remaining mixture. Spoon over the large dish, leveling the surface.

7 Put the small cakes, toddler and adult dishes on a baking sheet and bake in the oven for 8–10 minutes for the small cakes, 20 minutes for the ramekin and 30 minutes for the larger dish, until they are well risen and golden brown.

8 Dust the toddler's and adults' portions with confectioner's sugar and leave to cool slightly before serving with the custard. Warm the baby's apple mixture if desired and test the temperature before serving with the little cakes taken out of their paper cups.

TIP
If you can't get blackberries then use raspberries instead. There's no need to defrost before using as they will soon thaw when added to the hot apple.

Orange and Strawberry Shortcakes

6 tbsp all-purpose flour

4 tbsp butter

2 tbsp superfine sugar

grated zest of ½ orange

extra sugar, for sprinkling

For the Filling

6oz plain yogurt

1 tbsp confectioner's sugar

9oz strawberries

1 tsp Cointreau (optional)

2 sprigs of fresh mint

1 Preheat the oven to 350°F. Place the flour in a mixing bowl, cut the butter into pieces, and rub into the flour with your fingertips until the mixture resembles fine breadcrumbs.

2 Stir in the sugar and orange zest and mix to a dough.

3 Knead the dough lightly then roll out on a floured surface to ¼in thickness. Stamp out four 3½in flower shapes or fluted rounds with a cookie cutter and 12 small car, train or other fun shapes with novelty cutters, rerolling the dough as necessary.

4 Place on a baking sheet, prick with a fork and sprinkle with a little extra sugar. Bake in the oven for 10–12 minutes until pale golden, then let cool on the baking sheet.

5 For the filling, blend the yogurt with the sugar and wash and hull the strawberries. Pat dry. Reserve eight of the strawberries and process or blend the rest. Press through a strainer and discard the seeds.

6 For the adults, put 3 tbsp of the yogurt in a bowl and stir in the Cointreau, if using. Slice four strawberries and halve two, place on a plate and cover.

7 For the toddler, slice two of the strawberries and arrange in a ring on a small plate. Spoon 2 tbsp of yogurt into the center of the ring and serve with three of the small cookie shapes.

8 For the baby, stir 1 tbsp of the strawberry purée into the remaining plain yogurt and spoon into a small dish. Serve with one or two of the small biscuit shapes.

9 To complete the adults' portions, spoon the purée over two plates to cover completely.

10 Spoon the reserved yogurt over two biscuits, add the sliced strawberries and top with the other two cookies. Arrange on plates and decorate with halved strawberries and tiny sprigs of mint.

TIP
If you find shortbread difficult to roll out then chill for 20 minutes. Knead lightly and roll out on a surface dusted with flour, dusting the rolling pin too.

Warm Exotic Fruit Salad

oil, for greasing
2 tbsp brown sugar
1 ripe mango
1 kiwi
1 passionfruit
2 tbsp confectioner's sugar
12oz plain yogurt

1 Line a baking sheet with foil then trace two circles using a 1 cup ramekin, then trace another using a ⅔ cup ramekin. Lightly brush with oil. Sprinkle the sugar inside each marked circle in an even layer.

2 Broil the sugar discs for 2–3 minutes or until they have melted and caramelized. Let the discs cool on the baking sheet.

3 Slice the mango on either side of the central pit and then cut six thin slices for decoration, cutting away the skin. Cut the rest of the mango flesh from the pit, removing the skin, and finely chop one quarter, dividing between the baby bowl and a small ramekin. Coarsely chop the remainder and divide between the larger ramekins.

4 Peel the kiwi, cut in half lengthwise and then slice thinly. Reserve four half slices for decoration and divide the remaining fruit among the dishes, finely chopping the fruit for the baby and toddler. Cut the passionfruit in half and using a teaspoon scoop and place the seeds in the adults' dishes.

5 Stir the confectioner's sugar into the yogurt and mix 1 tbsp into the baby's portion. Spoon 2 tbsp yogurt over the toddler's dish and level the surface with a spoon.

6 Spoon the remaining yogurt into the other two ramekins, level the surface with a spoon and chill all of them until required.

7 When ready to serve, place the larger ramekins on two plates with the reserved mango and kiwi slices arranged around the sides. Peel the sugar discs off the foil and set on top of the adult and toddler portions. Serve immediately.

TIP
Traditionally the sugar topping on a brulée is made by sprinkling brown sugar over the top of the dessert and then broiling, or by making a caramel syrup and then pouring it over the dessert. Making the topping on oiled foil is by far the easiest and most foolproof way. Add the cooled sugar discs at the very last minute so that they stay crisp and you get that wonderful mix of crunchy sugar, velvety yogurt and refreshing fruit.

Plum Crumble

1lb ripe red plums

2 tbsp superfine sugar

For the Topping

1 cup all-purpose flour

4 tbsp butter, cut into pieces

2 tbsp superfine sugar

2 tsp chocolate chips

3oz marzipan

2 tbsp oatmeal

2 tbsp slivered almonds

plain yogurt or custard, to serve

1 Preheat the oven to 375°F. Wash the plums, cut into quarters and remove the pits. Place in a saucepan with the sugar and 2 tbsp water, cover and simmer for 10 minutes until just tender.

2 Drain and spoon six plum quarters onto a chopping board and chop finely. Spoon the plums into a small baby dish with a little juice from the saucepan.

3 Drain and coarsely chop six more of the plum quarters and place in a ⅔ cup ovenproof ramekin with a little of the juice from the saucepan.

4 Spoon the remaining plums into a 3⅔ cup ovenproof dish for the adults.

5 Make the topping. Place the flour in a bowl, rub in the butter and then stir in the sugar.

6 Mix 3 tbsp of the topping mixture with the chocolate chips then spoon over the ramekin.

7 Coarsely grate the marzipan and stir into the remaining topping with the oats and almonds. Spoon over the adults' portion.

8 Place the toddler and adult portions on a baking sheet and cook for 20–25 minutes until golden brown. Leave to cool slightly before serving. Warm the baby's portion if desired and check the temperature of the children's food before serving. Serve with plain yogurt or custard.

TIP
Ovens can vary in temperature: with convection ovens you may need to cover the adults' dish with foil halfway through cooking to prevent overbrowning.

Vary the fruits: cooking apples, peaches and pears also work well. If the plums are very tart you may need to add a little extra sugar.

Chocolate and Tangerine Trifle

½ chocolate jelly roll

3 tangerines

4 tsp sherry

2oz dark chocolate

1¼ cups ready-made custard

6 tbsp heavy cream

M & M's

1 Slice the jelly roll, halve one slice and put on a plate for the baby. Put a second slice into a ramekin for the older child and arrange the remaining slices in two dessert bowls for the adults.

2 Peel one tangerine, separate into segments and put a few on the baby plate. Chop the rest and add to the ramekin.

3 Peel the remaining tangerines, coarsely chop and add to the adults' bowls, sprinkling a little sherry over each.

4 Break the chocolate into pieces and melt in a bowl over a saucepan of hot water. Stir the melted chocolate into the custard.

5 Spoon 2 tbsp of the custard into a small bowl for the baby and arrange on the plate with the jelly roll and tangerines. Spoon a little more custard into the ramekin and then add the rest to the adult dishes, smoothing the surface.

6 Whip the cream until it just holds its shape. Add a spoonful to the ramekin and two or three spoonfuls each to the adults' dishes, decorating each dish with M & M's. Chill the trifles until serving.

TIP
Chocolate may be melted in the microwave in a microwave-safe bowl for 2 minutes on High (100%), stirring thoroughly halfway through cooking.

Some shops sell ready-made chocolate custard, buy this if available and you're short of time.

Vary the fruit depending on what is in season, sliced strawberries and orange or sliced banana and fresh or canned cherries also work well.

Apple Strudel

1lb cooking apples

2oz dried apricots

3 tbsp golden raisins

2 tbsp light brown sugar

2 tbsp ground almonds

1 tsp ground cinnamon

2 tbsp butter

3 sheets filo pastry, defrosted
 if frozen

confectioner's sugar, to dust

light cream, to serve

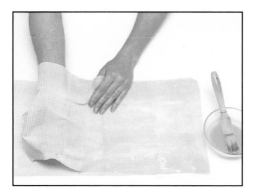

4 Carefully open out the pastry. Place one sheet on a work surface, brush with butter then cover with a second sheet of pastry and brush with more butter.

7 Brush a little of the butter over half of the third pastry sheet then fold the unbrushed half over the top to make a square. Brush again and cut into three equal strips.

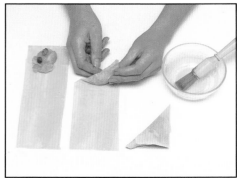

8 Put a spoonful of apple at the base of each strip then fold the bottom right-hand corner up and over the filling to the left side of the strip to make a triangle.

9 Continue folding the pastry to make a triangular pastry. Repeat with the other strips.

1 Preheat the oven to 400°F. Peel, core and chop the apples and place 5oz in a saucepan. Chop three apricots and add to the pan with 1 tbsp golden raisins, 1 tbsp sugar and 1 tbsp water. Cover and simmer for 5 minutes.

2 Chop the remaining apricots and place in a bowl with the remaining apples, raisins, sugar, ground almonds and cinnamon. Mix together well.

3 Melt the butter in a small saucepan or microwave in a microwave-safe bowl for 30 seconds on High (100%).

5 Spoon the uncooked apple mixture in a thick band along the center of the pastry.

6 Fold the two short sides up and over the filling and brush with butter. Fold the long sides up and over the filling, opening out the pastry and folding the pastry for an attractive finish. Place on a baking sheet and brush with a little butter.

10 Transfer to a baking sheet and brush with the remaining butter. Bake for 10 minutes, and the adults' strudel for 15 minutes, until golden and crisp. Dust with confectioner's sugar and cool slightly.

11 Spoon the remaining cooked apple mixture into a baby dish. Mash the fruit if necessary. Transfer the toddler's portion to a plate. Slice the strudel thickly and serve with cream.

TIP
Filo pastry is usually sold frozen in 10oz packs or larger. Defrost the whole pack, take out as much pastry as you need, then rewrap the rest and return to freezer as soon as possible.

Strawberry Pavlova

2 egg whites
4oz superfine sugar
½ tsp cornstarch
½ tsp wine vinegar
For the Topping
⅔ cup heavy cream
9oz strawberries
2 chocolate chips
green chuckles or gum drop

1 Preheat the oven to 300°F and line a baking sheet with non-stick baking paper.

2 Whisk the egg whites until stiff and then gradually whisk in the sugar 1 tsp at a time. Continue whisking until smooth and glossy.

3 Blend the cornstarch and vinegar and fold into the egg whites.

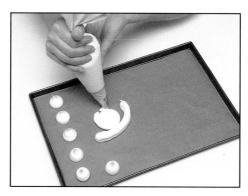

4 Spoon the mixture into a large pastry bag fitted with a medium-sized plain tube. Pipe six small dots for the baby and a snail for the older child with a shell about 2½in in diameter.

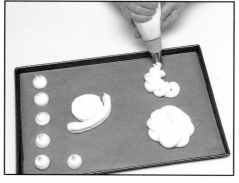

5 Pipe the remaining mixture into two 4in swirly circles and cook in the oven for 20–25 minutes or until firm. Lift the meringues off the paper and leave to cool.

TIP
For perfect meringues whisk the egg whites in a dry greasefree bowl. Remove any trace of yolk with a piece of shell and whisk until the peaks are stiff but still moist looking. Add sugar gradually and continue whisking until very thick. Meringues may be made 1–2 days in advance, if desired. Cover with wax paper and decorate just before serving.

6 Whip the cream until softly peaking and spoon over the two large meringues and the toddler's snail, reserving about 1 tbsp of cream for the baby.

7 Rinse, hull and slice the strawberries and arrange a few in rings over the snail. Place the snail on a plate and add chocolate eyes and a slice from a green chuckles or gum drop for the mouth.

8 Add some strawberries to the adult meringues then chop or mash a few extra slices and stir them into the reserved cream for the baby. Spoon into a small dish and serve with tiny meringues.

Poached Pears

3 ripe pears

1⅞ cup apple juice

1 tsp powdered gelatin

few drops of green food coloring

½ small orange, peel only

½ small lemon, peel only

2 tsp chopped candied ginger

1 tsp clear honey

1 tsp cornstarch

1 red licorice bootlace

2 small currants

1 raisin or large currant

½ candied cherry

1 Peel the pears leaving the stems in place. Cut a small circle out of the base of two pears and tunnel out the cores with a small knife.

2 Halve the remaining pear, discard the stem, scoop out the core and then put them all in a pan with the apple juice. Bring to a boil, cover and simmer for 5 minutes, turning the pears once.

3 Lift out the pear halves and reserve, cooking the whole pears for 5 minutes more or until just tender. Remove with a slotted spoon and place on a serving dish reserving the cooking liquid. Finely chop one pear half and put into a small dish for the baby. Reserve the other half pear for the toddler.

4 Pour half of the reserved apple juice into a bowl, place over a pan of simmering water, add the gelatin and stir until completely dissolved. Transfer to a measuring cup and pour half over the chopped pear and chill.

5 Stir a little green coloring into the remaining gelatine mixture, pour into a shallow dish or a plate with a rim for the toddler, and chill.

6 Cut away the peel from the orange and lemon and cut into thin strips. Add to the remaining apple juice with the ginger and honey and simmer over a gentle heat for 5 minutes until the peel is soft.

7 Blend the cornstarch with a little water to make a smooth paste, stir into the pan then bring the mixture to a boil and cook, stirring, until thickened. Pour over the whole pears and let cool.

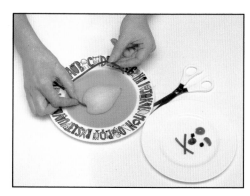

8 Place the toddler's pear, cut side down, on the green jelly. To make a mouse, add a piece of red licorice for a tail and two pieces for whiskers. Make two small cuts for eyes and tuck a currant into each slit. Add a raisin or large currant for the nose. Halve the cherry and use for ears. Serve slightly chilled with cream for the adults, if desired.

Peach Almond Tart

1½ cups all-purpose flour

6 tbsp butter

For the Filling

4 tbsp butter

¼ cup superfine sugar

1 egg

few drops of almond extract

⅔ cup ground almonds

2 tbsp apricot preserves

1 tbsp chopped candied citrus
   peel

14oz can peach slices in natural
   juice

1 tbsp slivered almonds

1 tbsp plain yogurt

confectioner's sugar, for dusting

crème fraîche or plain yogurt,
   to serve

1 Place the flour in a bowl, cut the butter into small pieces and rub into the flour with your fingertips until the mixture resembles fine breadcrumbs.

2 Stir in 6–7 tsp water and mix to a smooth dough. Knead lightly on a floured work surface and roll out thinly.

3 Lift the pastry over a rolling pin and use to line a 7in flan dish pressing down against the sides of the dish. Trim the top.

4 Reroll the trimmings and cut out twelve 2in circles with a fluted cookie cutter, pressing into sections of a mini muffin pan. Chill the pastry for 15 minutes.

5 Preheat the oven to 375°F. Line the large flan dish with wax paper and fill with baking beans. Cook in the preheated oven for 10 minutes then remove the baking beans and paper and cook the shell for 5 minutes more.

6 Meanwhile make the filling: cream together the butter and sugar in a bowl until light and fluffy. Beat the eggs and almond extract together then gradually beat into the creamed sugar. Stir in the ground almonds and set aside.

7 Divide the preserves among the small and large tarts, spread it into a thin layer in the large tart and sprinkle with candied peel. Spoon all of the almond mixture over the top and level the surface.

8 Drain the peaches and set aside three slices for the baby. Cut three slices into chunks and divide among six of the small tarts, leaving six with just preserves.

9 Arrange the remaining peaches over the top of the large tart and sprinkle with slivered almonds.

10 Cook the small tarts for 10 minutes and the large tart for 25 minutes until the filling is set and browned. Dust the large tart with confectioner's sugar and let cool.

11 Process or blend the reserved peaches for the baby. Mix with the plain yogurt and spoon into a small dish. Serve with two plain preserves tarts.

12 Arrange a few fruity tarts on a plate for the toddler. Cut the large tart into wedges and serve with crème fraîche or plain yogurt for the adults. Test the temperature of the children's tarts before serving.

Honey and Summer Fruit Mousse

2 tsp powdered gelatin

1¼lb bag frozen mixed berries, defrosted, or fresh berries, cleaned and trimmed

4 tsp superfine sugar

1¼lb container plain yogurt

⅔ cup whipping cream

5 tsp clear honey

1 Put 2 tbsp cold water in a cup and sprinkle the gelatin over making sure that all the grains of gelatin have been absorbed. Soak for 5 minutes, then heat in a saucepan of simmering water until the gelatin dissolves and the liquid is clear. Cool slightly.

2 For baby, process or blend 2oz of fruit to a purée and stir in 1 tsp sugar. Mix 3 tbsp plain yogurt with 1 tsp sugar in a separate bowl.

3 Put alternate spoonfuls of plain yogurt and purée into a small dish for the baby. Swirl the mixtures together with a teaspoon. Chill until serving.

4 For the toddler, process or blend 2oz fruit with 1 tsp sugar to a purée. Mix 4 tbsp plain yogurt with 1 tsp sugar then stir in 2 tsp fruit purée.

5 Stir 1 tsp gelatin into the fruit purée and 1 tsp into the yogurt mixture. Spoon the fruit mixture into the base of a glass and chill until set.

6 For the adults, whip the cream until softly peaking. Fold in the remaining plain yogurt and honey and add the remaining gelatin. Pour into two 1 cup molds and refrigerate until set.

7 Spoon the remaining yogurt mixture over the set fruit layer in the serving glass for the toddler and chill until set.

8 To serve, dip one of the dishes for the adults in hot water, count to 15, then loosen the edges with your fingertips, invert onto a large plate and, holding mold and plate together, jerk to release the mousse and remove mold. Repeat with the other mold. Spoon the remaining fruits and some juice around the desserts and serve.

TIP
If you have a small novelty mold you may prefer to set the toddler's portion in this rather than a glass or plastic container.

Make sure the gelatin isn't too hot before adding to plain yogurt or it may curdle.

Hot Fruit Salad with Ginger Cream

2 oranges

4 bananas

2oz pitted dates

2 tbsp golden raisins

2 tbsp butter

3 tbsp brown sugar

2 tbsp Cointreau or brandy

vanilla ice cream, to serve

For the Ginger Cream

⅔ cup heavy cream

1 tbsp chopped candied ginger

grated zest of 1 orange

3 Peel and slice the bananas. Coarsely chop the dates. Arrange a few orange segments, slices of banana, pieces of date and a few raisins on a plate for the baby.

5 Stir the Cointreau or brandy into the pan, bring to a boil then quickly light with a match. Spoon the fruit into a serving bowl as soon as the flames subside. Serve the adults' flambéed fruit with ginger cream and the toddler's portion with ice cream. Test the temperature of the toddler's portion before serving.

1 First make the ginger cream: whip the cream until it just holds its shape, then finely chop the ginger and stir into the cream with the orange zest. Spoon into a small serving dish.

4 Melt the butter in a skillet, add the remaining fruit and sauté for 2 minutes, then stir in the sugar and cook for 2 minutes, until lightly browned. Spoon a few pieces of fruit into a bowl for the toddler.

TIP
Flaming dishes look so spectacular but are really very easy to do. The secret is to add the spirit to hot liquid, bring the liquid back to a boil then quickly light it with a match and stand back. The flames will subside in a minute or two. But if you are at all worried they can be quickly extinguished by covering the pan with a lid or baking sheet.

2 Cut a slice off the top and bottom of each orange and cut the remaining peel and pith away in slices. Cut into segments.

INDEX
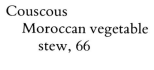

ACKNOWLEDGEMENTS

- The Department of Health
- National Dairy Council Nutrition Service
- Dr Nigel Dickie from Heinz Baby Foods
- The British Dietetic Association
- The Health Visitors' Association
- Broadstone Communications for their invaluable help supplying the Kenwood equipment for recipe testing and photography
- Cosmo Place Studio for hand-painted china plates, bowls and mugs
- Tupperware for plain-colored plastic bowls, plates, feeder beakers and cups
- Cole and Mason for non-breakable children's ware
- Royal Doulton for Bunnykins china
- Spode for blue and white Edwardian Childhood china

PICTURE CREDITS

The publishers would like to thank the following
for additional images used in the book:

Key: t = top; b = bottom; l = left; r = right.

Bubbles: pages 8 b, 11 t (Lois Joy Thurston); page 9 t (Nikki Gibbs);
pages 14 t, 13 t (Ian West); 15 br (Jacqui Farrow).
Lupe Cunha: page 8 t.
Reflections/Jennie Woodcock: pages 15 br, 9 b, 10 bl br.
Timothy Woodcock: page 11.

MODELS

The publishers would like to thank the following children and
adults for being such wonderful models: Maurice Bishop,
Andrew Brown, Penny and Chloe Brown, Daisy May Bryant,
April Cain, Helen and Matthew Coates, Cameron Gillis,
Jamie Grant, Sandra and George Hadfield, Ted Howard,
Emily Johnson, Huw and Rhees Jones, Key, Stephen, Charlie
and Genevive Riddle, William Lewis, Sadé Walsh, Lionel and
Lucy Watson, Lily May Whitfield, Philippa Wish, James Wyatt.